THE ROLE OF MONEY

History and Use | Economics

Social Studies Fourth Grade Non Fiction Books

Children's Money & Saving Reference

BIZ HUB
business | investing

First Edition, 2020

Published in the United States by Speedy Publishing LLC, 40 E Main Street, Newark, Delaware 19711 USA.

© 2020 Biz Hub Books, an imprint of Speedy Publishing LLC

Biz Hub Books are available at special discounts when purchased in bulk for industrial and sales-promotional use. For details contact our Special Sales Team at Speedy Publishing LLC, 40 E Main Street, Newark, Delaware 19711 USA. Telephone (888) 248-4521 Fax: (210) 519-4043. www. speedybookstore.com

10 9 8 7 6 * 5 4 3 2 1

Print Edition: 9781541949911
Digital Edition: 9781541951716

See the world in pictures. Build your knowledge in style.
www.speedypublishing.com

TABLE OF CONTENTS

A man wondering where money comes from

4

Do you like to spend money? Do you receive an allowance? Do you ever wonder where money comes from? Can you imagine living in a world where money is not used? That might be hard to imagine since money has been around for over four millenia, that is four thousand years!

This book talks about how people used to 'buy' or get things without using money, how and why money came to be, how money is produced, the uses of money and where money is kept.

WHAT DID PEOPLE USE AS PAYMENT BEFORE MONEY?

It may be hard to imagine that at one time in history, people did not use money as the means through which they acquired goods. Before people had money, they relied on trading items with each other. This is a system called bartering.

Native Americans bartering goods

Bartering works when one person has something that s/he can trade with another person in exchange for the item or goods that the other person has.

For example, if a carpenter was hungry and wanted some food, the carpenter could go to a farmer or a fisherman and see if the farmer or fisherman wanted to exchange their goods, crops or fish, for something that the carpenter made.

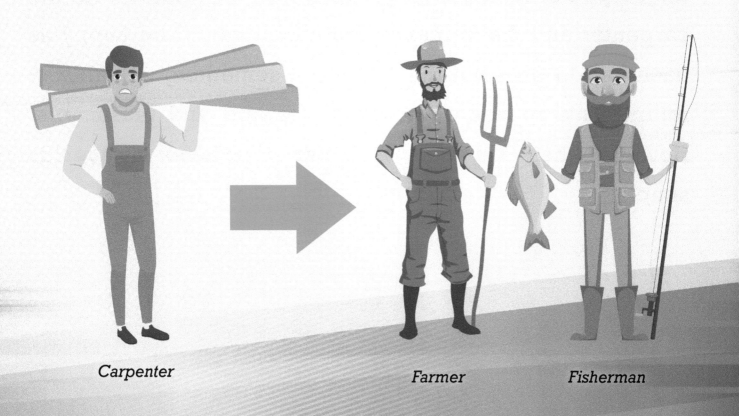

Carpenter

Farmer

Fisherman

If the farmer or fisherman needed a piece of furniture that the carpenter made, then goods would be traded. Both the carpenter and the farmer or fisherman would be happy as each had to give but they both got something valuable in return. This sounds quite straightforward and reasonable. However, there are times when bartering is not always this simple.

11

THE PROBLEMS
IN BARTERING

One problem was that it was not always possible to trade or barter in a way that was even or fair. Here is an example of might happen; a carpenter offers a fisherman a chair in exchange for some fish. The fisherman agrees to accept the chair and in return decides on a certain type of fish to be traded in exchange for the chair.

What if the chair is not made of strong wood or it is not the style that the fisherman wants? What if the carpenter thinks that the quality of the chair is greater than the quality or quantity of the fish that are offered in exchange for the chair? When these things happened, it was difficult to reach an agreement on what was a fair trade.

In trading, it can be difficult to agree on what is fair.

Another example in how bartering was difficult was that there was not always an equal need for goods. For example, sometimes, there were more fisherman or farmers in an area than carpenters. In that case, the carpenter could not meet the demand of the fisherman and farmers. Also, the carpenters themselves only needed so much food, then the farmers and fisherman were left with extra food that they were unable to trade.

The problem which seemed to be the one
which was the most challenging was the
effect of population growth.

A concept of a
population growth

As the population grew, people started to travel. When the people reached their destination, they needed new things such as accommodation and food.

It was not possible to carry their own personal goods in the hopes of being able to barter them successfully to find what they needed to meet their needs. Also, some goods were not the type that would last for long periods of time.

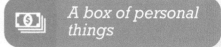
A box of personal things

Obviously, a trading system which involved the direct exchange of goods for goods had its limitations.

 Bartering of goods for goods

Therefore, another form of exchange had to be developed. The new form or medium of exchange was money.

The new form or medium of exchange was money

FORMS OF
MONEY

Although the need for money was realized, a new problem came with it. Different places used different things as money. Basically, people started to use what happened to be available in their local areas.

2 daler copper plate money, 1742

For example, shells, stones, especially those with holes put in the middle of them, and the teeth of whales were used as money.

 Brass vintage cowrie shells. They were used as money in ancient China

 Rai, or stone money circular stone disks carved out of limestone, quarried on several of the Micronesian islands

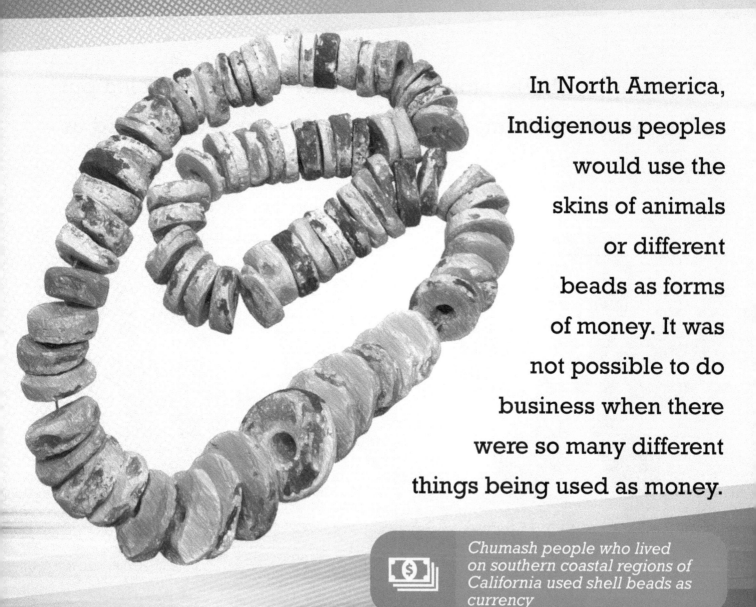

In North America, Indigenous peoples would use the skins of animals or different beads as forms of money. It was not possible to do business when there were so many different things being used as money.

Chumash people who lived on southern coastal regions of California used shell beads as currency

People soon discovered that money would have to be made of something which could be valued and widely used. It would also have to be something that everyone considered to be valuable enough to be accepted as money.

Exhibition of the history of money, Santa Marinella

2 SANTA MARINELLA (ROMA), 1927

Roma, età repubblicana (IV-III secolo a.C.)

1. Lingotto in bronzo (framm.)

Serie pesante
Bifronte imberbe / Mercurio
2-3. As
4-5. Semis
6-11. Triens

Serie pesante
Apollo / Apollo
13-14. As
15-16. Triens

Serie
Dioscuro / Apollo
17. As
18. Semis

It was decided that some precious metals would be used: gold, silver and copper. Since gold was not as common or widely available, it was the most valuable of the three metals.

Gold silver and copper was used to make as money

From these metals,
it was much easier
to make a monetary
system that worked.
Firstly, the value
of the precious
metals was
accepted by
everyone.

 Gold, silver and copper nuggets

Secondly, metal can be molded into a variety of sizes with each size weighing a different amount. Each different piece could be given a different value or worth.

Old coins found on archaeological excavations in India

Thirdly, as metal is a hard substance, after the money was produced and put into circulation, it had the ability to last for a very long time. It was durable!

Ancient coins of the Roman Empire

Fourthly, compared to some other forms of goods that were used in trade, such as items of furniture, money was much easier to carry from one place to another. Moreover, even though the pieces of metal may be small and easy to transport, their value would not diminish.

 Money was much easier to carry from one place to another

Fifthly, metal, especially gold, will always be considered valuable because there is only so much of it on Earth.

 Four sets of Gold Coins of Vima Kadphise, India, Kushan Empire

MONEY IN THE FORM OF COINS AND PAPER

Coins were made long before paper was chosen as a form of money. Precious metals have been used as a material for coins for more than two thousand and five hundred years.

Ancient Greece Coins. Greek Gallery, Altes Museum, Berlin, Germany

Coins are still used today but they are not made of precious metals anymore. The difference between the coins that were first used as money and the coins today is that today the coins only have the value of the amount of money that they represent. They do not have value in the material that is used to make them.

Various American coins

For example, a five-cent coin is only worth five cents today. This is unlike the value of the coins when they were first made. When the coins were first made, in addition to the value that was stamped on the coin, the material itself, the precious metal, was valuable.

 One nickel coin (five cents)

After people started to use coins for a while, they realized that too many coins were heavy to transport.

Bag of coins were heavy to transport

This led to the creation of paper money which started to be made more than eight-hundred years ago.

Song Dynasty Jiaozi, the world's earliest paper money

Although the paper did not have much value itself, the value of each denomination of paper money became determined by the value that was assigned to it at the time of printing.

The front (or face) of a 1779 fifty-five dollar bill of Continental currency

In other words, a one-dollar bill would only have the value of one-dollar.

One-dollar bill

The new money which included both coins and paper was given the name *currency*. It was much more convenient, lighter in weight and easy to carry around. Having a few coins was not too inconvenient.

Paper money and coins are much more convenient to carry around

Using paper money and coins have made it easier to do trade and business

The combination of coins and paper proved to be much better than the type of money that it replaced. People from different places were able to trade and do business with each other much easier than they had been before.

MONEY AS
WE KNOW IT
TODAY IN THE
UNITED STATES

BUREAU OF ENGRAVING AND PRINTING

The United States Bureau
of Engraving and Printing
headquarters building

The United States Government oversees the production of money. The department that is responsible for printing money is the Bureau of Engraving and Printing.

This department has two locations from which it prints money: Washington, D.C. and Fort Worth, Texas.

 Bureau of Engraving and Printing.Washington, District of Columbia DC, USA

 Bureau of Engraving and Printing, Fort Worth

Once the money is made, it is sent to one of the many locations, known as branches, of the Federal Reserve Bank. This is a special government owned bank that has many branches in different states. In addition to having newly printed currency, any of these bank branches can exchange old and tattered bills or coins for new ones.

 Federal Reserve building in Washington, DC

THE ROLE OF
BANKS

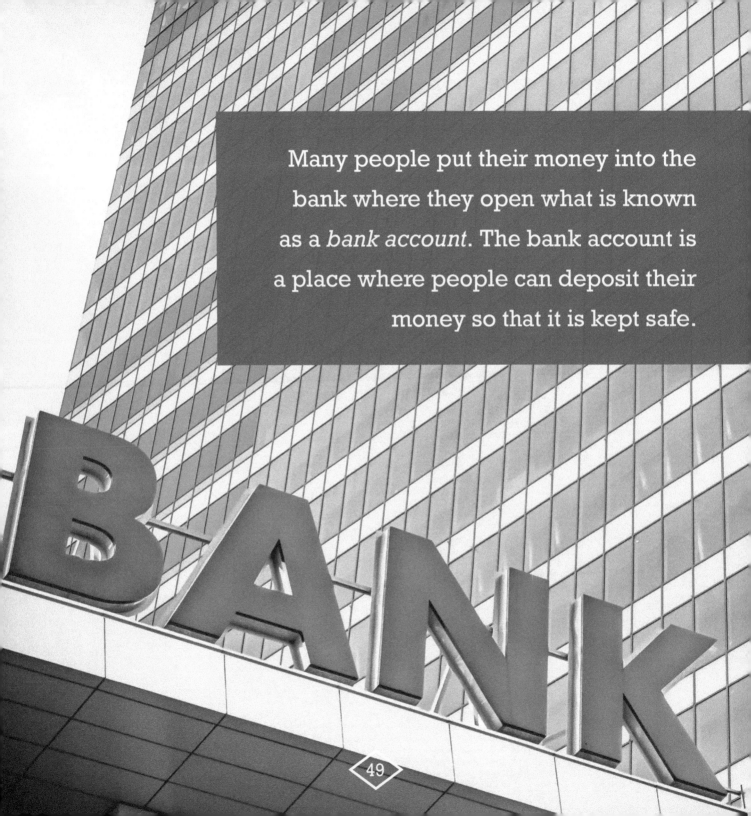

Many people put their money into the bank where they open what is known as a *bank account*. The bank account is a place where people can deposit their money so that it is kept safe.

When people have a job, their employer often pays them through direct deposit; that is the money they earn at their job is put right into their bank account.

 A man holding his savings account passbook

People can take out or withdraw their money as they wish. Their money is used to pay bills and buy goods, for example.

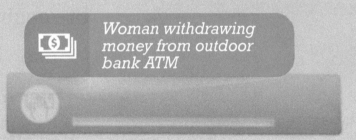
Woman withdrawing money from outdoor bank ATM

Because it is not always convenient or safe to carry large amounts of cash, many people use other things in place of money. Some examples are credit cards, debit cards or checks.

 Many people use credit card, debit card or even checks

To have a credit card, a person or applicant applies to a credit card company. There is often a fee that the person pays to the company to have the card.

 Bank Credit Card Application

APPLICATION FORM:
Credit Card

Section 1. FOR BANK
Credit Card Nu

Section 2. Applicant Information

Surname

First Names

Title

Mr

Once the credit card company approves the applicant's credit card application, the applicant is issued a credit card.

CREDIT CARD

1234 5678 1012 3456

0000

VALID DATES 00/00

NAME SURNAME

A man holding his credit card

The credit card is used instead of cash to buy goods or services. The credit card company will pay for the goods or services and the person later pays the credit card company the amount that was spent.

A woman paying using a credit card at a supermarket

If the person does not pay the money within a certain amount of time, the credit card company will charge the person interest. That is, in addition to the cost of the goods or services bought, the person must pay extra money to the credit card company because the original price was not paid in full within the required amount of time.

An image showing a statement account of the credit card

Debit Card

1234 5678 9012 3456

CARDHOLDER

Best Card

 A debit card comes with a person's bank account

A debit card usually comes with the account that a person opens with the bank. The person can use the debit card instead of cash to pay for goods or services.

Unlike a credit card, a debit card takes the money directly from the person's account to pay for something. If the person does not have enough money in the account, the debit card will be denied at the shop or place of business where the person tried to make a purchase.

Debit card used in purchasing goods

A check comes in the form of a document on a piece of paper in a small rectangular shape. It is used by people to make a purchase instead of using cash. The understanding is that the buyer is promising that s/he has enough money in the bank to cover the amount of money written on the check.

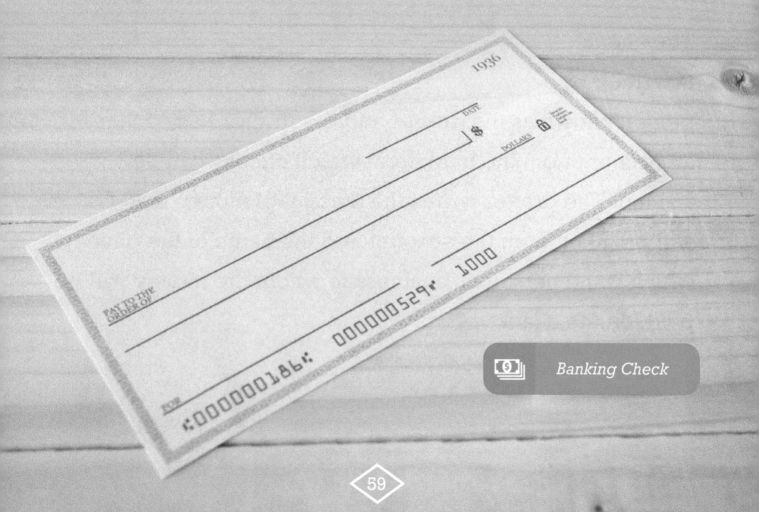

Banking Check

The check
is written by a
person known as the drafter and the drafter has
an account from the bank from which checks can be
written. The drafter writes the amount of money that
will be taken from the account and the name of the payee,
which is the person or business to whom the money will be
paid, on the check.

Man signing his check

The bank will take the money from the person's account to pay for the item or service.

Man using check as payment

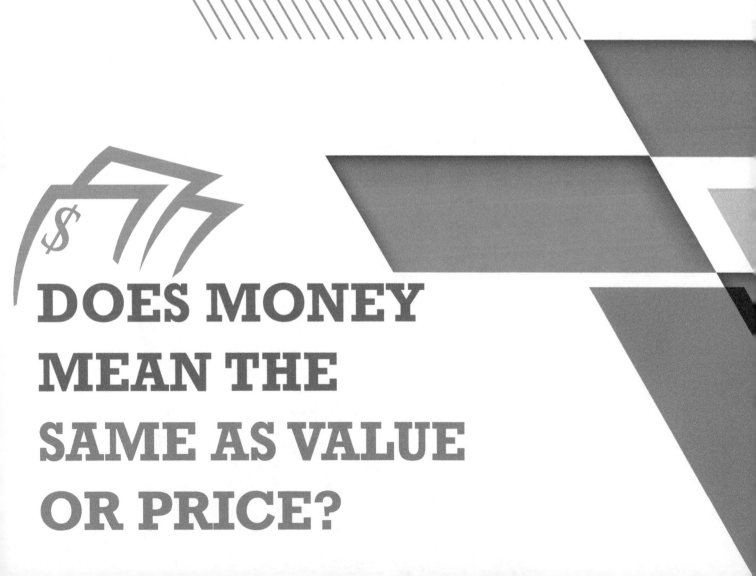

DOES MONEY MEAN THE SAME AS VALUE OR PRICE?

Money is used to pay for a good or service which people consider to be of value or importance. It is necessary to have money because it is the medium of exchange for goods or services.

A lady using money to pay for her groceries

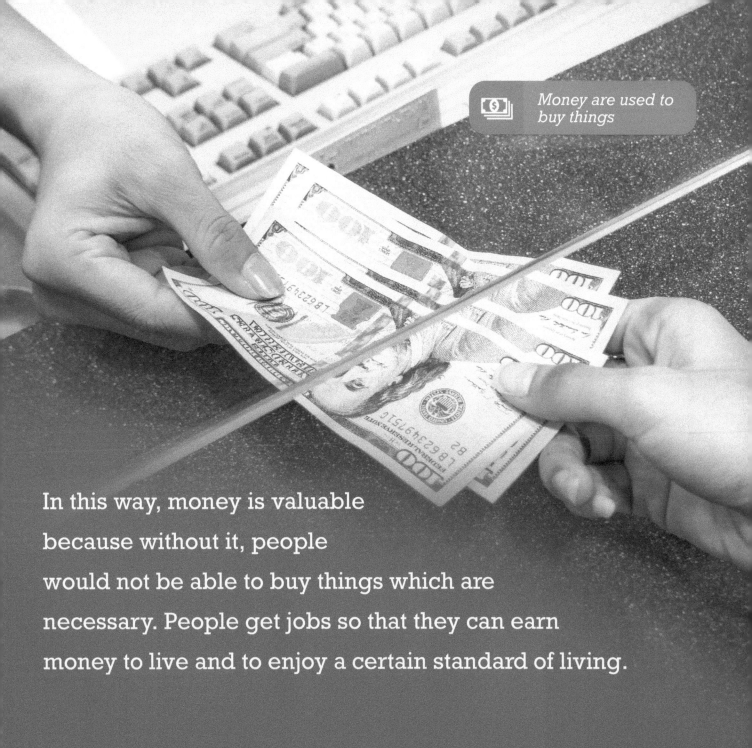

In this way, money is valuable
because without it, people
would not be able to buy things which are
necessary. People get jobs so that they can earn
money to live and to enjoy a certain standard of living.

DEMAND

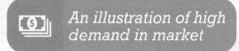
An illustration of high demand in market

Price refers to how much a good or service costs. It is determined by the demand, or in other words, how many people want the goods or services.

Demand is the quantity of a good that consumers are able to purchase at various prices during a given period of time.

It is also influenced by how expensive it is to manufacture the product or in the case of a service how much value is put on that service. Will the service save someone's life or just provide the person with enjoyment for a short period?

Man buying an expensive car

Although money is the medium of exchange in the world today, it does not determine the price or value of something.

Worldwide exchange of goods and services

Money is used worldwide as the main form of exchange to receive goods or services. It replaced the system of bartering goods in exchange for other goods or services.

SUMMARY

In the United States, money is printed in a special bank that is owned by the government. People make money by having jobs. Most people keep their money in banks. People often use debit cards, credit cards, or checks instead of carrying large sums of cash.

Visit

www.speedypublishing.com

to download Free Baby Professor eBooks and view our

catalog of new and exciting Children's Books

Lightning Source UK Ltd.
Milton Keynes UK
UKHW051525020121
376250UK00002B/31